AMERICA'S GREATEST TEAMS

THE LOS ANGELES LAKERS

Sloan MacRae

PowerKiDS press™
New York

Published in 2010 by The Rosen Publishing Group, Inc.
29 East 21st Street, New York, NY 10010

First Edition

Editor: Amelie von Zumbusch
Book Design: Greg Tucker
Photo Researcher: Jessica Gerweck

Photo Credits: Cover Shutterstock.com; cover (Kareem Abdul-Jabbar) Mike Powell/Allsport/Getty Images; cover (Kobe Bryant), p. 5 Melissa Majchrzak/NBAE via Getty Images; cover (Magic Johnson), pp. 7, 15, 17, 22 (middle) Andrew D. Bernstein/NBAE/Getty Images; cover (Wilt Chamberlain), pp. 13, 22 (top) Wen Roberts/NBAE/Getty Images; p. 9 Noel Vasquez/Getty Images; p. 11 © Bettmann/Corbis; pp. 19, 22 (bottom) Robert Mora/NBAE/Getty Images; p. 21 Noah Graham/NBAE/Getty Images.

Library of Congress Cataloging-in-Publication Data

MacRae, Sloan.
  The Los Angeles Lakers / Sloan MacRae. — 1st ed.
     p. cm. — (America's greatest teams)
  Includes index.
  ISBN 978-1-4042-8132-5 (library binding) — ISBN 978-1-4358-3398-2 (pbk.) —
ISBN 978-1-4358-3399-9 (6-pack)
  1. Los Angeles Lakers (Basketball team)—Juvenile literature. 2. Basketball—California—Los Angeles—
Juvenile literature. I. Title.
  GV885.52.L67M33 2010
  796.323'640979494—dc22
                                            2009009504

Manufactured in the United States of America

CONTENTS

DYNASTIES

A sports team is said to be a dynasty when it wins several **championships** in a short amount of time. Most teams never have a single dynasty in their history. However, the Los Angeles Lakers have had several dynasties over the years. Their success made the Lakers one of the most **popular** teams in the National Basketball Association, or NBA.

Some of the biggest names in basketball have played for the Lakers. George Mikan was the NBA's first great superstar. Wilt Chamberlain, Kareem Abdul-Jabbar, and Shaquille O'Neal were so popular that they appeared in Hollywood movies. Many sports **experts** believe that present Laker Kobe Bryant is today's greatest basketball player.

Kobe Bryant is one of today's top basketball stars. He was named the most valuable player, or MVP, in 2008.

HALL OF FAMERS

As many sports do, basketball has a Hall of Fame. The Basketball Hall of Fame is a **museum** in Springfield, Massachusetts. It honors the greatest basketball players in history.

Many big stars never become Hall of Famers. However, there are quite a few former Lakers in the Hall of Fame. Jerry West, Wilt Chamberlain, and Kareem Abdul-Jabbar are all there. Sports experts think that Kobe Bryant will someday be in the Hall of Fame. The hall also honors great basketball coaches. Coaches Bill Sharman and Pat Riley won places there for their success in leading the Lakers. These Hall of Fame players and coaches created the Lakers dynasties.

Hall of Famers Pat Riley (left, standing) and Magic Johnson (right) helped make the Lakers a powerful force in the 1980s.

HOLLYWOOD'S HOME TEAM

The Lakers are based in Los Angeles, California. Hollywood and the movie **industry** are there, too. Therefore, many **celebrities** and movie stars are Lakers fans. Famous movie star Jack Nicholson is often seen at Lakers games.

The Lakers' colors are purple and gold. The team plays in an arena called the Staples Center. It is named after Staples, a company that sells office supplies. The Lakers share the Staples Center with other Los Angeles basketball teams. The Los Angeles Clippers play there. The Sparks, a team in the Women's National Basketball Association, or WNBA, play there, too. The Staples Center also **hosts** rock concerts and hockey games.

You can often see famous movie stars, such as Zac Efron (left) and Leonardo DiCaprio (right), at Lakers games.

LAND OF 10,000 LAKES

Los Angeles does not have many lakes, so people often wonder why its team is called the Lakers. However, the team was not always based in Los Angeles. The Lakers began in Michigan, as the Detroit Gems. In 1947, businessmen Ben Berger and Morris Chalfen bought the Gems and moved the team to Minneapolis, Minnesota. Minnesota has lots of lakes. It is called the Land of 10,000 Lakes. The owners renamed the team the Lakers.

A talented player named George Mikan joined the Lakers in 1947. Mikan became a basketball star. He led the Lakers to win three NBA championships in the 1950s. The Lakers were the NBA's first dynasty.

George Mikan was the first very tall basketball star. Mikan stood 6 feet 10 inches (2 m) tall.

CALIFORNIA

In the 1940s and 1950s, California had no NBA teams. In the late 1950s, Bob Short bought the Lakers. Short thought that a basketball team that was based in California would be popular. He moved the Lakers to Los Angeles in 1960.

The Lakers played well in the 1960s and 1970s. Lakers Wilt Chamberlain, Jerry West, and Elgin Baylor became superstars. The team reached the NBA championship six times in the 1960s but often lost to the Boston Celtics. The Celtics became the Lakers' biggest **rivals**. In 1972, the Lakers won 33 **consecutive** games. No other American **professional** basketball, football, hockey, or baseball team has had a winning **streak** this long.

Wilt Chamberlain (center) joined the Lakers in 1968. His height and skill earned him the nickname the Big Dipper.

IT'S SHOWTIME

The Lakers **drafted** Earvin Johnson in 1979. He was such a talented player that he became known as Magic Johnson. Johnson had one of the greatest **rookie** seasons ever. He and superstar Kareem Abdul-Jabbar led the Lakers into the championship series against the Philadelphia 76ers.

During the 1980s, the Lakers were known as the Showtime Lakers because their games were so much fun to watch. Coach Pat Riley joined the team in 1981 and helped Los Angeles reach even more championship series. When the Lakers won the championship in 1987, Riley said they would do it again next year. He was right, and the Lakers were once again a dynasty.

Magic Johnson (left) was named MVP three times. His teammate Kareem Abdul-Jabbar (right) was the MVP six times.

NOTHING LASTS FOREVER

The stars of the Showtime Lakers **retired** in the late 1980s and early 1990s. Los Angeles reached the Finals again in 1991, but they lost to Michael Jordan and the Chicago Bulls. No dynasty can last forever, and the Lakers dynasty was coming to an end. Jordan and the Bulls became the **dominant** dynasty of the 1990s.

The Lakers had been good for a long time, but they were no longer one of the NBA's greatest teams. That began to change in 1996 when two new players joined the team. Fans did not yet know it, but Shaquille O'Neal and Kobe Bryant would soon return the Lakers to greatness.

Sadly, the Lakers lost the 1990–1991 NBA season championship series to the Chicago Bulls, four games to one.

SHAQ

Shaquille Rashaun O'Neal's first and middle names together mean "little warrior," but he is anything but little. He stands over 7 feet (2.1 m) tall and weighs more than 300 pounds (136 kg). O'Neal quickly became a star for the Lakers. He would later become one of the top NBA scorers of all time.

In 1999, the Lakers hired coach Phil Jackson. Jackson had already helped the Chicago Bulls become a dynasty. Could he do it again in Los Angeles? The Lakers won the championship during Jackson's first season as coach. O'Neal and new superstar Kobe Bryant then led the Lakers to two more consecutive championship wins. People began talking about a Los Angeles dynasty again.

Shaquille O'Neal (right) is often just called Shaq. He is one of the most famous NBA players ever.

KOBE

The Lakers traded O'Neal to the Miami Heat after the 2003–2004 season. The Lakers' owners decided to build a team around Kobe Bryant. Bryant is one of today's most dominant basketball players. Many experts believe he is the greatest player since Michael Jordan. Bryant is so well known that he often goes by his first name. The Lakers' owners filled the rest of the team with good players, such as Lamar Odom, Pau Gasol, and Derek Fisher, who can help their superstar.

Today, Kobe and the Lakers are one of the best teams in the NBA. Fans hope that they will begin another dynasty in Los Angeles.

Bryant (left) is the Lakers' biggest star. Other strong players on the team include Pau Gasol (right). Gasol joined the Lakers in 2007.

LOS ANGELES LAKERS TIMELINE

1947

The Detroit Gems become the Minneapolis Lakers.

1950

The Lakers win the NBA's very first championship.

1960

The Lakers move to Los Angeles.

1972

The Lakers break a record by winning 33 consecutive games. They also win the championship.

1968

Wilt Chamberlain joins the Lakers.

1975

Kareem Abdul-Jabbar joins the Lakers.

1979

The Lakers pick Magic Johnson in the NBA draft.

1996

Shaquille O'Neal (right) and Kobe Bryant join the Lakers.

1985

The Lakers finally beat the Celtics to win a championship.

2002

The Lakers win the NBA Finals for a third consecutive time.

GLOSSARY

CELEBRITIES (seh-LEH-breh-teez) Famous people.

CHAMPIONSHIPS (CHAM-pee-un-ships) Games held to decide the best, or the winner.

CONSECUTIVE (kun-SEH-kyuh-tiv) In a row, or back to back.

DOMINANT (DAH-mih-nent) Top.

DRAFTED (DRAFT-ed) Selected for a special purpose.

EXPERTS (EK-sperts) People who know a lot about a subject.

HOSTS (HOHSTS) Supplies a home for something.

INDUSTRY (IN-dus-tree) A business in which many people work and make money by producing something.

MUSEUM (myoo-ZEE-um) A place where art or historical pieces are safely kept for people to see and to study.

POPULAR (PAH-pyuh-lur) Liked by lots of people.

PROFESSIONAL (pruh-FESH-nul) Someone who is paid for what he or she does.

RETIRED (rih-TY-urd) Gave up an office or job.

RIVALS (RY-vulz) People or teams who try to get or do the same thing as one another.

ROOKIE (RU-kee) Having to do with a new major-league player.

STREAK (STREEK) A long line of wins or losses.

INDEX

WEB SITES

Due to the changing nature of Internet links, PowerKids Press has developed an online list of Web sites related to the subject of this book. This site is updated regularly. Please use this link to access the list:
www.powerkidslinks.com/teams/laker/